# 101 Super Bad Jokes for Nurses

## Jokes to make you groan, smile, and roll your eyes!

This is a "just for fun" text from the semi-twisted mind of a recovering marketer and father. All jokes made within this text come from the author OR open source material that can not be attributed to any single person or source.

# Dedication/Apology

This book is dedicated to all the nurses out there who sit on the front lines of health and make us feel better. Administering these jokes will bring a smile to others, as well as, a moan or a groan to the reader as well.

Just be warned upfront - if you repeat these jokes too often, your friends, co-workers, and patients will REALLY start to wonder about you.

I would also like to thank (and apologize to) my family for putting up with me all these years. Your patience in listening to my dribble has been instrumental in my determination to come up with these ever more clever and horrendous jokes that I am now sharing with you all.

Finally, to my boat family and friends - thank you for everything!

You guys are the best!

**What complications arose when the hospital hired a Roman nurse?**

*She only issued the IV to bed number 4.*

What inspires a nurse to move at the speed of light?

*A bed alarm or fresh coffee in the breakroom*

Why does the infectious disease ward at the hospital have the fastest Wi-Fi?

*Because it has all the hot spots!*

# What do you tell a nurse when she administers an injection painlessly?

*Good jab*

# What did the forgetful nurse say?

*I have a joke on amnesia, but I forget how it goes...*

# Why did the nurse need a red crayon?

*In case she needed to draw blood*

# Did you hear about the nurse who injured his entire left side?

*Don't worry, he's all right now*

What did the nurse say to the man who fainted at the airport terminal?

*I think you might have a terminal illness*

# What did the nurse say when a boy told her he stood on a LEGO?

*"Try to block out the pain"*

# What did the balloon say to the nurse during the routine check-up?

*I am feeling a bit light-headed*

# Why didn't one nurse find the other nurse's joke funny?

*She had an
irony deficiency*

# What did the cookie say to the nurse?

*I am feeling crumby*

# What do transplant nurses hate?

*Rejection*

# Why was the nurse feeling mad?

*He ran out of patients*

# How was the nurse's advice on Q-tips received?

*It went inside one ear and out the other!*

**What was the reaction of the patient who broke three ribs while lifting?**

*He felt like he had a weight on his chest*

**What did the bucket tell the nurse when she asked what happened?**

*"I'm here to see the doctor, I seem to have a pail face"*

# How do you know when a nurse is having a bad day?

*He won't stop needling people*

Why did the robot ask the nurse to call the doctor immediately?

*Because it had a virus*

What did the guy say when the nurse informed him that she was about to deliver the baby?

*"We want our baby to keep its liver, please!"*

# What did the witch say to the nurse?

*I have an appointment with the doctor for all my dizzy spells*

What did the nurse advise the patient who got heartburn after eating a birthday cake?

*She advised him to take the candles off first!*

**Why did the senior nurse appreciate the new nurses' work?**

*Her alphabetized list of organ donors was well organ-ized.*

What did the nurse say to the tonsil?

*"You should get dressed, the doctor is going to take you out now"*

# Why was the nurse found to be so nervous?

*Because it was his first shot in the hospital*

# Why are nurses afraid of the outdoors?

*Too much poison IV*

What did the nurse say when a patient said, "I've swallowed a spoon"?

"Sit down, and please don't stir..."

**What were the nurses discussing at the medical conference?**

*One of them asked, "Heard about the germ...? Oh never mind, I shouldn't be spreading it around."*

What did the nurse say when a patient who had multiple vegetables stuck to his body ask, "What is wrong with me?"

"You're not eating properly"

What did the nurse say when the patient said he felt like a carrot?

*The nurse advised him not to get himself in a stew*

# What did Dracula say to the nurse?

*Please call the doctor - I can't stop coffin!*

# Why did the patient identify the nurse as a curtain?

*Because she was seen pulling herself together...*

# What did the blood donor say to the nurse?

## "I feel super tired, this is such a draining process"

**What did the patient ask when the nurse informed him that he had a-cute appendix?**

*"Compared to whom?"*

# Why did Mr. Peanut go to the hospital?

*Because he was a-salted*

# What did the rope say to the nurse?

*I have an appointment with the doctor - I've been in knots all week!*

What did the nurse reply when someone asked, "Does an apple a day keeps the doctor away?

Yes, if you aim it nicely

# What is it called when a hospital runs out of maternity nurses?

## *A mid-wife crisis!*

# What did the nurse say to the rocket ship?

*It's time for your booster shot*

What did the nurse say when a patient said he swallowed a watch?

*"These medicines will help pass the time"*

# What did the nurse say to the patient's family?

*"I didn't have the heart to tell you that the doctor wasn't able to get the organ donor yesterday."*

# Why did the banana say to the nurse?

*I am here to see the doctor, I am not peeling well!*

# What did the pillow say to the nurse?

*Please help,
I feel stuffed!*

How many nurses do you need to change a lightbulb?

*It takes just one nurse, but she needs 20 seconds to change it and another 45 minutes to chart it*

**Why was the ambitious nursing student collecting skulls?**

*So she could get ahead of everyone*

What did the senior nurse advise the young nurse about her first injection?

*"Just give your best shot"*

What did the new night nurse reply when the senior nurse asked her about nitrates?

*"Are they cheaper in comparison to day rates?"*

What did the nurse say to the patient who fainted at the airport terminal?

*"You have been diagnosed with a terminal illness"*

# What did the mattress say to the nurse?

*"I think I have spring fever"*

"Knock knock"

"Who is there?"

"Urine"

"Urine who?"

"Urine in trouble if you forget to do the bedside report"

"Knock Knock"

"Who is there?"

"Yoda"

"Yoda who?"

"Yoda, the best nurse ever, thanks for taking care of me!"

"Knock, knock!"

"Who is there?"

"Nightshift"

"Night shift who?"

"Um, nevermind, it's not that important, it can wait till dayshift"

The teacher asked a group of nurses what is bacteria?

*One of them replied, "Is it a back door to the cafeteria?"*

I decided not to vaccinate my daughter...

*I let the nurses do it since they have more experience*

Why were the nurses so suspicious of the patient?

*He had a lot of secret-ion.*

**Heard about the man who cut his fingers using an electric saw?**

*When a nurse asked about the cut-off fingers, the man said, "I didn't have anything to pick them up with."*

# Acupuncture

## *What's the point?*

# Why did the nurse keep a bandage by their side?

*For a quick "wrap-up"!*

Why did the nurse bring a ladder to work?

*To elevate the patient's spirits!*

A ghost asked, "Nurse, can you tell me what the X-ray of my head shows?

"Absolutely nothing!" she replied

Did you hear about the two podiatrists who left the practice?

*They became arch-enemies*

A small boy swallowed some coins and was taken to a hospital. When the nanny asked how he was doing...

*...the nurse said, "No change yet."*

# The nurse who can smile when things go wrong...

*Is probably going off duty*

Heard about the guy who kept thinking he was a bell?

*The nurse asked him to go home and give her a ring if the feeling persists...*

How do night nurses feel when they think about their early days at the hospital and want to go back?

*They feel nursetalgic.*

What did the nursing student ask when the teacher started talking about D&C?

*"Is this chapter about where Washington is?"*

# Why was the nurse tip-toeing around the medicine cabinet?

*She was scared of waking up the sleeping pills*

What did the nurse say to the complaining patient?

"I have a lot of patience, but you're testing it!"

Nurse pops her head into the doctor's office.....
"Doctor, there's an invisible man in the waiting room."

Doctor: 'Tell him I can't see him.'

A nurse walks into a bar and orders a beer. "Are you coming to our big Halloween party?" the bartender asks.

"Yes, I've already planned my costume. I'm going to come as a horrible monster made entirely out of blood," the nurse says.

*"I'm going to be a hemogoblin."*

I kept trying to play hide-and-seek when I was in the hospital...

*...but the security kept finding me in the ICU*

A man is in a hospital and waits for a nurse to come. After a long time, the nurse comes in and says "Sorry I kept you waiting"

*He replies "No worries. I'm patient"*

# Why did the nurse bring a magnifying glass to work?

*To help with "examine-ations"!*

# What did one nurse say to the other nurse during a long shift?

*"We make a great 'pair-a-medics'!"*

# Why did the nurse bring a deck of cards to work?

## To "deal" with any emergencies!

What did the nurse say to the medicine maker when he got sick?

*Lemme give you a taste of your own medicine...*

# What do you call a nurse who loves to sleep?

*"Coma-tose!"*

A priest, rabbi, and minister all had to go to the hospital. Turns out, they got alcohol poisoning from going to the bar so much.

# Why did the nurse refuse to give a sponge bath?

*They didn't want to "wipe away" the patient's identity!*

Did you read about the night nurse who was squashed by a load of books?

*The only person she could blame was hershelf*

**Do you know why that man sent the nurse an X-ray of his entire chest?**

*He wanted to tell her that his heart was indeed in the right place*

# All bleeding stops:

## *Eventually*

# Never upset a pediatric nurse.

*They have very little patients*

I was in the hospital and asked the nurse if I could do my own stitches.

She said "suture self"

My younger brother made so many rash decisions he decided to become a dermatologist

# What did the nurse say to the patient who kept cracking jokes?

*"You're really tickling my funny bone!"*

# What do you call a nurse who can juggle?

*A multitasker on "medical rounds"!*

# What do you call a nurse who can play the piano?

*A "key" caregiver!*

**Don't mess with nurses, they get paid to stab people with very sharp objects.**

When I got my 3rd shot this afternoon. I asked the nurse if she knew what the chair I sat in was called to which she responded:

*"it's a booster seat"*

My best friend's name is Pam and she's pretty low-key and great to be around...

*She often goes by Loraze Pam, Diaze Pam, or Clonaze Pam.*

# How does Thor's nurse treat him back to health?

*She Norses him through the night*

What do you call a nurse who can do magic tricks?

A "sleight-of-hand" healer

What did the nurse reply when someone asked, "Does an apple a day really keep the doctor away?"

"Yes, if you aim it nicely."

# What do you call a nurse who can't find their pen?

*"Ink-capable" of writing prescriptions!*

# What's a nurse's favorite dance move?

## The "IV shuffle"!

# What's a nurse's favorite type of humor?

*"Ward" jokes!*

What did the custodian say when he jumped out of the closet in front of the nurses?

*"SUPPLIES!!"*

# Why are nurses always so calm?

*Because of patients*

What do you call a nurse with a great sense of humor?

The "laughing gas" of the hospital!

**What's a nurse's favorite kind of coffee?**

*Java – Just Another Vital Assignment!*

# What's next?
# Why more of course!

## Volumes #2 and #3
## will be out soon  :)

Printed by Amazon Italia Logistica S.r.l.
Torrazza Piemonte (TO), Italy

52928701R00063